SUDBURY HALL

Derbyshire

Acknowledgements

This is a revised and considerably amplified version of the 1982 guidebook, which in turn was based on the original guide by John Cornforth and Christopher Wall, first published in 1970. I am particularly grateful to Lord Vernon, who gave permission for Gervase Jackson-Stops to examine George Vernon's Day Book, and who kindly commented on the present text; to John Cornforth for his advice on John Fowler's work at Sudbury; to James Doody, who allowed me to see his unpublished research on George Devey; and to Robert Parker and his staff at Sudbury. Thanks are also due to Emil Godfrey, John Hodgson, Cherry Ann Knot, Nicholas Taylor, Adrian Tinniswood and the staff of the RIBA Drawings Collection. The picture entries are based on those written by St John Gore, amplified from Alastair Laing's notes.

The Vernon Estate Papers are on deposit in the Derbyshire County Record Office in Matlock. Architectural drawings for the unexecuted proposals by Salvin, Nesfield and Barry and for Devey's scheme are in the house and the Sudbury Estate Office. There are also related drawings by Barry and Devey in the RIBA. The fullest account of the house is that by Christopher Hussey in *Country Life*, 15, 22, 29 June 1935, pp. 622–7, 650–6, 682–7. Particularly useful were Jill Allibone's monographs on Salvin and Devey, William Warren Vernon's *Recollections of Seventy-two Years*, 1917, and John Cornforth's 'Sudbury Revisited', *Country Life*, 10 June 1971, pp. 39–49. The Harestaffe poem is printed in *Journal of the Derbyshire Archaeological and Natural History Society*, x, February 1888, pp. 71–147.

Oliver Garnett

Photographs: Country Life Picture Library p. 47; National Trust pp. 44, 45, 46; National Trust Photographic Library back cover, p. 32; NTPL/Andrew Butler pp. 1, 5, 6, 7, 33; NTPL/Andreas von Einsiedel front cover, pp. 4 (bottom), 8, 9, 13, 14, 15, 17, 19, 20, 21, 23, 25, 27, 28, 38, 40, back cover; NTPL/John Hammond pp. 4 (top), 11, 16, 18, 24, 31, 36, 37, 41, 42 (right), 43; NTPL/Angelo Hornak p. 29; Rijksmuseum-Stichting, Amsterdam p. 39; Royal Commission on the Historical Monuments of England p. 35; Southampton Art Gallery/Bridgeman Art Library, London p. 42 (left).

Reprinted with corrections 1985, 1988, 1991, 1992, 1995; reprinted 1994, 1996, 1997, 1999, 2003; revised 1998, 2002

Designed by James Shurmer

Phototypeset in Monotype Bembo Series 270 by SPAN Graphics Ltd, Smallfield, Surrey (SG1250)

Print managed by Centurion Press Ltd (BAS) for National Trust Enterprises Ltd, 36 Queen Anne's Gate, London SW1H 9AS

(*Front cover*) The Great Hall

(*Title-page*) The cartouche over the entrance door on the north front was carved by William Wilson

(*Back cover*) George William Henry Vernon, 7th Baron, aged 4 in 1858 at Sudbury Hall

CONTENTS

SUDBURY HALL

*(Above)
George Vernon,
the builder of
the house;
by J. M. Wright
(no. 19; Saloon)*

*Grinling Gibbons's
limewood carving
of fish in the
Drawing Room*

Sudbury is largely the creation of George Vernon (1635/6–1702), 'a prudent young man, sober and active', as he was described by a contemporary. He succeeded to the estate in 1660 and almost immediately began to rebuild the old manor house of his ancestors, probably to his own designs. Of all the great houses built in Charles II's reign, Sudbury Hall is one of the most idiosyncratic: a marriage of old-fashioned Jacobean features (particularly on the exterior) with carved stone, wood and plasterwork in the up-to-date classical style of Sir Christopher Wren's City churches. Some of the magnificent interior decoration was not completed until 30 years after the house was begun, and as time progressed, provincial craftsmen, like the plasterer Samuel Mansfield and the carver William Wilson, were replaced by more fashionable London men, including Edward Pierce, Grinling Gibbons, Thomas Young and the plasterers Bradbury and Pettifer. The finishing touches came only in the 1690s, with Louis Laguerre's Baroque murals and painted ceilings to the Staircase, Saloon and other rooms.

Sudbury has remained the home of the Vernon family ever since. Few changes have been made to the house, apart from the addition of a service wing on the east side, designed by George Devey in 1873–83, which replaced an earlier Victorian wing by Anthony Salvin. W. S. Gilpin, Joseph Paxton and William Andrews Nesfield all advised on the gardens in the nineteenth century, and the terraces and lake on the south side of the house are mostly of this date.

Sudbury was given to the Treasury in 1967, in part-payment of duties after the death of the 9th Lord Vernon, and was subsequently transferred to the National Trust, which commissioned the late John Fowler to redecorate several of the principal rooms.

The north front

TOUR OF THE HOUSE

The Exterior

THE ENTRANCE (NORTH) FRONT

The first impression is of Sudbury's huge scale and of a slightly frowning look, particularly on a dull day. Like Hardwick, it is a house that appears to grow upwards, but whereas Hardwick seems all of a piece, one can see at Sudbury a development of ideas as the walls rose before George Vernon's eyes. Tracing the entries in his account book, from the early 1660s to his death in 1702, this sense of development comes over still more clearly as load after load of bricks appears on the scene, stone for the window frames and quoins, followed by lead, glass and timber. Some of his payments are for features clearly recognisable today: for instance, Thomas Phillips was paid 16s on 20 October 1668 for '16 big stones for cullomes', and it is presumably these that can be seen on the frontispiece of the house today. Two years later George Vernon made

an agreement with the carver and master-mason William Wilson 'to finish mee ye two frontispiece of my house, on ye top of ye front and backe porch as draughts' for £35; 'The cuttinge ye boys over ye porch & ye Ionick heads & frutage hee refers to mee & ye bores heade,' all to be done for £7. Wilson also did the carving on the cupola and in 1671 George Vernon bought 174 stones for it at 2d a time.

It is no surprise to find stone mullion-and-transom windows still in use at this date, for the earliest record of sash-windows in England (at Whitehall Palace) dates only from 1662. But there are other distinctly old-fashioned features of the entrance front at Sudbury which are harder to explain: the diapered brickwork, possibly a reference to the fretwork of the Vernon arms; the carved stone ornaments over the ground-floor windows (again incorporating the Vernon fret), which are close to Jacobean strapwork in spirit; the curious form of the window above the porch, with an arch support-

The north front, with Devey's service wing on the left

The south front

ing a pair of circles, almost like spectacles, and the similar windows with pairs of ovals on either side. The latter may owe something to the carver William Wilson, who incorporated similar window-frames in his designs for St Mary's, Warwick.

The segmental pediments above and below the porch window, the elaborate cartouches which they frame, and the garlanded Ionic columns at first-floor level, are features Wilson almost certainly derived from French and Dutch pattern books. The upper cartouche, for instance, with its cornucopias and palm fronds, closely resembles a print by Jean Barbet of the 1630s, which Inigo Jones and John Webb had earlier used in the Queen's House, Greenwich, and at Wilton. The Ionic capitals are, on the other hand, likely to be based on Van Campen's Stadhuys (or Town Hall) at Amsterdam, built in the 1640s and equally well-known to English architects and craftsmen through engravings at this date. The great 'panelled' chimneystacks and the central cupola, crowned by a golden ball to reflect the sun's rays and act as a beacon for travellers, show a more up-to-date knowledge of Sir Roger Pratt's houses, such as Coleshill in Berkshire (destroyed in 1952) and Kingston Lacy in Dorset.

In the mid-eighteenth century, one important modification was made to the main block by the builder's grandson, the 1st Lord Vernon: the wooden balustrade round the central 'platform' of the roof (which can be seen in John Griffier's picture, illustrated on p. 37) was removed, lessening the impact of the hipped roof, and giving greater prominence to the cupola and chimneys than was originally intended. The dormer windows were also altered at this date. George Devey was responsible for adding the present stone balustrade at parapet level in 1873.

THE EAST WING

The east wing to the left of the entrance front was designed as servants' quarters by George Devey in a neo-Jacobean style for the 6th Lord Vernon between 1873 and 1883, when much of the decayed seventeenth-century stonework on the two main façades was renewed.

THE GARDEN (SOUTH) FRONT

One of the most noticeable features of the south front is a change in the colour of the brickwork. This was probably caused by George Vernon employing a great number of local brickmakers. As opposed to the drama of the entrance front, with deep shadows cast by the projecting wings and by Wilson's porch with its superimposed orders, the south side of the house is relatively static in character. Again the development of Vernon's taste is evident as the eye travels upwards – a result of the long-drawn-out building operations recorded in his account books. The string course between ground and first floors, decorated with triglyphs and rosettes, is so tentative in its classicism as to be reminiscent of Robert Smythson's ornament at Bolsover and Hardwick, built half a century earlier.

The central window is another idiosyncratic composition, perhaps due to the influence of William Wilson; yet the latter's carving in the pediment above – cornucopias and palm fronds supporting a Baroque shield of arms – is in the spirit of Wren's City churches and the contemporary buildings of Robert Hooke. The porch, with its great central arch, was originally open; the present glazing dates from 1834, and the stone steps leading up to it probably date from the same time.

The Interior

THE ENTRANCE PASSAGE

The Entrance Passage links the north and south fronts, and, like a medieval screens passage, divides the Great Hall and the other principal state rooms on the right, from the smaller family rooms and servants' quarters on the left. The stone paving, quarried at Breadsall, was put down in 1671.

PICTURES

(All pictures are painted on canvas unless otherwise stated.)

1 JOHN GRIFFIER the Elder (1645–1718)
View of the South Front of Sudbury and its Original Formal Garden
Signed: *JOHN GRIFFER FECIT*
George Vernon's new house and garden were almost complete when this view was painted around 1690. It shows the original wooden balustrade that crowned the roof of the house, the church on the left, and, on the right, Vernon's barn and stables, built in 1661 and 1664 respectively. It also depicts the elaborate formal garden to the south of the house, with a long fish-pond in the foreground, where the lake is today.

The Entrance Passage

2 ENGLISH, mid-eighteenth-century
George, 2nd Lord Vernon as a Boy (1735–1813)
Known as the 'Hunting Lord', he enjoyed exercising his hounds on the south lawn. He inherited Sudbury in 1780.

3 ENGLISH, mid-eighteenth-century
Mary Vernon, later Mrs Anson, as a Girl (b.1739)
Daughter of the 1st Lord Vernon and Mary Howard. In 1763 she married George Adams, who took the name of Anson in 1773 on inheriting Shugborough in Staffordshire (also now the property of the National Trust).

SCULPTURE

ENGLISH
Frances Warren, Lady Vernon (1784–1837)
Wife of the 4th Lord Vernon, she brought the lucrative Poynton cotton mills and coalfields into the family.

ENGLISH
Augustus, 6th Lord Vernon (1829–83)
See no. 10 (Great Hall).

FURNITURE

Eighteenth-century Chinese black-lacquered screen.

Set of William and Mary high-back chairs in the style of Daniel Marot (*c*.1663–1752).

Dutch walnut-veneered longcase clock by Gerrit Bramer of Amsterdam.

Bracket clock by Charles Frodsham presented by the workers at the Poynton and Worth collieries to the 7th Lord Vernon on his marriage in 1885.

The mirror carved with winged putti, grapes and scrolling acanthus leaf decoration was converted from a seventeenth-century picture frame.

THE GREAT HALL

The Entrance Passage and Great Hall may originally have been one large room and have been divided only in the late eighteenth or early nineteenth century. An early ground plan of the house seems to show this arrangement; in 1872 the retired Sudbury agent, Mr Chawner, referred to 'the division between Entrance and large Dining Hall

The Great Hall

erected previous to my Agency'; and there appear to be awkward joins in the plasterwork frieze at the corners of the dividing wall. On the other hand, the plasterer Samuel Mansfield's account of August 1675 lists 44 yards of 'Cornish' (cornice) in the Hall (which corresponds with the present shape of the room) and also refers to work in 'the hall passage'. The stone paving also came from Breadsall.

The room was used by the family for large formal dinners and other entertainments. It was redecorated in 1969 by the National Trust.

CHIMNEYPIECE

The giant marble chimneypiece may have been inserted in the early 1900s. What was presumably its predecessor, which was even higher and flanked by stone columns, can be seen in the portrait of the 7th Lord Vernon at the foot of the Great Staircase.

PICTURES

4 Studio of Sir JOSHUA REYNOLDS, PRA (1723–92)
King George III (1738–1820)
The originals of this and its pendant (no. 5) were painted for the Royal Academy in 1779.

5 Studio of Sir JOSHUA REYNOLDS, PRA (1723–92)
Queen Charlotte (1744–1818)

6 Sir THOMAS LAWRENCE, PRA (1769–1830)
Henry, 3rd Lord Vernon (1747–1829)
On marrying Elizabeth Nash, the illegitimate daughter of Sir Charles Sedley, 2nd Bt, in 1779, he took the name of Sedley until he succeeded to the Vernon title on his half-brother's death in 1813. Painted soon after he succeeded, in his peer's robes.

OVER CHIMNEYPIECE:

7 LOUIS LAGUERRE (1663–1721)
An Allegory of Industry and Idleness
Mural, c.1691, in plaster frame.
On the left Industry digs his ground. Behind are a field of ripe corn, a good house with a smoking bakehouse chimney and a pigeon-cote. On the right Idleness lies in rags. His house is ruinous, his cart broken and his trees dead. Between is the god Saturn, representing the passage of time. To Industry he offers a cornucopia, to Idleness a bunch of thorns.

8 Sir THOMAS LAWRENCE, PRA (1769–1830)
Edward Vernon, Archbishop of York (1757–1847)
Younger son of 1st Lord Vernon and Martha Harcourt; in 1831 took the name of Harcourt on in-

heriting that family's estate. He was a distinguished clergyman, becoming Archbishop of York in 1807.

9 Sir JAMES JEBUSA SHANNON, ARA (1862–1923)
George Francis, 8th Lord Vernon (1888–1916)
Signed and dated 1903
He is wearing the uniform of a page at the coronation of Edward VII in 1902. He fell ill while on active service in Gallipoli, and died in Malta.

10 ANGELO ROMAGNUOLI (active 1879–96)
Augustus Henry, 6th Lord Vernon (1829–83)
Signed and dated 1884
Succeeded his father, in 1866; married in 1851 Harriet, daughter of the 1st Earl of Lichfield. He was responsible for the restoration of the house and the building of the east wing in the 1870s.

11 JULES LEFEBVRE (1836–1912)
Frances Lawrance, Lady Vernon (d.1940)
Signed and dated 1883
Daughter of Francis Lawrance of New York; married the 7th Lord Vernon in 1885.

SCULPTURE

OVER DOORS:

Charles II (1630–85)
Plaster

MICHAEL RYSBRACK (1694–1770)
Admiral Edward Vernon (1684–1757)
Marble
See no. 16 (Great Staircase). Rysbrack also carved Vernon's monument in Westminster Abbey.

IN CORNERS:

ENGLISH
Isabella Ellison, Lady Vernon (1805–53)
First wife of the 5th Lord Vernon.

ENGLISH
George, 5th Lord Vernon (1803–66)

FURNITURE

A rosewood-veneered and ebony stand decorated with ormolu and brass inlay, and with a green malachite top, probably by the leading cabinetmaker and dealer George Bullock, c.1815. It supports a candlestand (converted for electricity), which is said to have been brought back by Admiral Sir John Borlase Warren from St Petersburg, where he served as ambassador in 1802.

Two pairs of early Victorian mahogany serving-tables carved with Egyptian waterleaf and papyrus decoration.

An Allegory of Industry and Idleness; mural by Louis Laguerre, c.1691 (no. 7; Great Hall)

CERAMICS

ON SIDE-TABLES:

Table-centre of six Sèvres biscuit porcelain hunting figures, presented to the 6th Lord Vernon by the French government in recognition of his work to alleviate famine among French farmers in 1870–1.

Nineteenth-century Meissen vases encrusted with flowers and decorated with birds.

ON CHIMNEYPIECE:

Eighteenth-century Japanese Imari plates.

THE GREAT STAIRCASE

Perhaps the finest staircase of its date *in situ* in an English country house, this vast rectangular space with its two broad flights of stairs provided a suitably grand link between the Great Hall and the Great Stairhead Chamber (now the Queen's Room) and the Long Gallery on the first floor. It may have been designed by George Vernon himself. A plan of the room is clearly annotated in his hand and has on the back calculations of the cost of 'moulding, turning, framing & finishing', as well as the charge to be expected from 'Mr Peirce for carvinge – without ye Pinaples'. Edward Pierce's final bill for the Staircase, amounting to £112 15s 5d, was paid in 1676, by which time the idea of pineapples had presumably been abandoned in favour of the present baskets of fruit, which could be moved at night and replaced by candelabra or lanterns.

Edward Pierce (*c.*1630–95) was one of the most talented of all the craftsmen to emerge in the rebuilding of London after the Great Fire in 1666, and 'was much employed by Sir Chr. Wren in his Carvings & Designs', according to the eighteenth-century antiquary George Vertue. The son of a painter of the same name, his training is obscure, but as well as sculpture and carving he practised architecture and decorative painting. He was mason-contractor for four of Wren's City churches, and supplied carved woodwork for six of them, including the magnificent reredos for St Matthew, Friday Street (now at Polesden Lacey in Surrey).

BALUSTRADE

Pierce's staircase balustrade deserves to be ranked among the carver's finest achievements: the giant scrolling acanthus pattern, daringly pierced and undercut, gives a sense of movement to the architecture that is essentially Baroque. Its inspiration may well have been the luxuriant acanthus of his father's series of engravings, entitled *Designs for Friezes*, first published in 1640, but reissued by the younger Pierce in 1668, and again about 1680.

The balustrade is carved in limewood, the baluster rail in pine, and the flower baskets in elm. Over the years, the carving had become so clogged by brown paint and varnish that its quality was partly obscured. During the restoration of the house by the National Trust, successive layers of paint were removed from the balustrade, revealing a white scheme which John Fowler believed to be the original and to which he decided to return. However, a memorandum written in 1872 by Mr H. Chawner, Lord Vernon's agent, was subsequently discovered, which reads: 'This fine staircase was about the year 1834 painted white. . . . All the doors etc. were also painted white at that time'. It was probably this scheme which Fowler's scrapes uncovered.

PLASTERWORK

The plasterwork of the ceiling, the cove and the underside of the stairs was carried out by James Pettifer in 1675 and is as spectacular as Pierce's carving. Similar acanthus scrolls, garlands of fruit and flowers, palm branches and chains of husks, give a feeling of extraordinary richness – once again reminiscent of Wren's City churches.

CEILING PAINTINGS

In the early 1690s, nearly twenty years after the completion of the staircase, George Vernon commissioned Louis Laguerre (whose work he had probably encountered at Chatsworth) to fill Pettifer's blank plasterwork panels with figurative paintings. On the soffit below the landing is *Leda and the Swan* and under the slope of the stairs a figure of *Juno*. The subject of the ceiling is the *Rape of Oreithyia*. The story, which comes from Ovid's *Metamorphoses*, Book VI, is that Boreas, the North Wind, courted the nymph Oreithyia, but was repeatedly rejected. Finally he lost his temper and raped her.

DOORCASE

The massive architectural doorcase at the foot of the stairs leading to the Saloon is also thought to date from the early 1690s, and to be the work of another craftsman from Chatsworth, the carver Thomas Young; he was paid £25 in 1691 for unspecified carving at Sudbury.

DECORATION

The warm yellow colour of the walls, dating from the Trust's restoration of 1969, was suggested by John Fowler. While not a consciously historical choice, it resolves to a large extent the contrast between the sombre Baroque colouring of Laguerre's paintings and the delicate plasterwork frames in which they are contained, picked out in the same off-white as the staircase balustrade.

It is regretted that visitors cannot use the Staircase as it is felt that the strain imposed would be too great for it and the plasterwork might suffer.

PICTURES

12 JULIAN STORY (1857–1919)
George William Henry, 7th Lord Vernon (1854–98)
Signed and dated 1891
Succeeded his father in 1883, but lived away from Sudbury in his later years, when the house was rented out. He is shown standing in front of a fireplace that may once have been the Great Hall.

13 ENOCH SEEMAN (1694–1745)
Martha Harcourt, Lady Vernon (1715–94)
Third daughter of the Hon. Simon Harcourt and sister of the 1st Earl Harcourt; married the 1st Lord Vernon as his third wife in 1744.

14 ? MICHAEL DAHL (1656/9–1743)
Arabella Vernon, Lady Rushout (d.1705)
Daughter of Sir Thomas Vernon and sister of George Vernon's third wife; married Sir James Rushout, 2nd Bt, of Northwick Park in 1699/1700.

15 ENOCH SEEMAN (1694–1745)
Thomas, 6th Lord Howard of Effingham (1682–1725) and his Wife, Mary Wentworth
The parents of Mary Howard, first wife of the 1st Lord Vernon.

16 CHARLES PHILLIPS (1708–47)
Admiral Edward Vernon (1684–1757)
Second son of James Vernon, secretary of state under William III, and a cousin of the Sudbury Vernons.

(Opposite page) The Great Staircase

His long naval service, which began in 1701, reached its peak with his celebrated victory at Porto Bello in 1739 and ended with his being cashiered in 1746 after verbal attacks on the Admiralty. He stopped the Navy issuing neat spirits to seamen, substituting a less intoxicating mixture of rum and water which came to be known as 'grog' (Vernon's nickname was 'Old Grog', derived from his 'grogram' [*gros grain*: 'coarse grain'] boat-cloak).

17 After PIETRO DA CORTONA (1596–1669)
The Rape of the Sabines
A copy of the picture in the Capitoline Museum, Rome.

54 ROBERT EDGE PINE (1742–90)
John, Earl of Warren and Surrey, giving his answer to the King's Justices on the Enforcement of the Statute of Quo Warranto, 1278
In 1278 Lord Warren was interrogated under the statue of *Quo Warranto* as to the title by which he held his lands. He is alleged to have brandished a rusty sword, saying: 'Here, my Lord, is my warrant. My ancestors coming in with William the Bastard

won their lands with the sword, and with the sword I will hold them against all comers.' He won the sympathy of the nobles and the King accepted his claim.

For notes on the outer Staircase pictures see p. 26, where the Landing is described.

FURNITURE

Eighteenth-century giltwood console table supported by an eagle, with a grey-veined marble top, in the style of William Kent (1685/6–1748).

THE SALOON

In George Vernon's day, this was known as the Parlour and was probably his principal dining-room. For years the room has been almost empty of furniture and used for entertaining rather than for everyday living. In the nineteenth and twentieth centuries the children's Christmas party was held

The Saloon

Edward Pierce carved the swags of fruit and flowers below the portraits in the Saloon

here, with a tree in the middle of the room. Whatever it may now lack in contents, it makes up for in superb decoration.

Though at first sight one of the most pleasantly unified and architectural rooms at Sudbury, at least four different stages can be traced in the development of the Saloon. Like the Staircase, it combines a most elaborate plasterwork ceiling by Bradbury and Pettifer with superb carved woodwork round the walls by Edward Pierce, of 1675 and 1678 respectively. Also like the Staircase, it was made more fully Baroque in the 1690s by the insertion of Laguerre's ceiling painting representing the *Four Seasons* within the central shallow dome. In the mid-eighteenth century, the 1st Lord Vernon altered the effect of Pierce's wainscot by lengthening the pedimented 'tabernacles' round the walls, so as to frame a series of full-length family portraits; and finally in the nineteenth century, the 5th Lord Vernon introduced the jasper chimneypiece (which he acquired in the south of France) and the overmantel mirror, as well as commissioning the London firm of decorators Howard & Sons to redecorate the room about 1864. The painting and gilding of the walls, thought not to have been touched since then, were cleaned in 1968, when the ceiling was repainted to complement their subtle tones. At the same time the floor, which had been polished, like those in all the other reception rooms, was stripped to reveal the oak boards.

CEILING PLASTERWORK

Bradbury and Pettifer's plasterwork, with its amazingly three-dimensional acanthus and palm branches, incorporating diminutive cupids and giant shells, reaches a crescendo in the oval wreath of flowers at the centre – a fitting frame for Laguerre's later *Seasons*, and most likely the reason for the artist's choice of subject. The plasterwork panel over the window probably shows four of the seven virtues: Faith and Charity crowning Hope, with Justice above.

WALL-CARVING AND PANELLING

Pierce's 'tabernacles' with their segmental pediments are likely to be derived from another of Jean Barbet's designs, pirated by the London publisher Robert Pricke in his collection of engravings, *The Architect's Store-House* (1674).

The richest carving is kept for the overdoors, framing the portraits of George Vernon and his third wife, but here the influence is clearly Dutch: the garlands bound with snaking ribbons are closer to Artus Quellin's stone-carving for the Amsterdam Town Hall, and the work of his most famous pupil, Grinling Gibbons.

The panelling, made from trees on the estate, was put up by Thomas Johnson in 1677.

LIGHTING

The rare giltwood chandeliers of *c.*1740 were acquired by the 1st Lord Vernon and retain the pulleys, cords and weight mechanism that enabled them to be lowered for lighting. Similar tasselled cords are illustrated in the 1762 edition of Chippendale's *Director*.

The gilded lead wall brackets decorated with saracens' heads are of about 1730.

PICTURE

(Starting over the door to the Staircase and continuing in a clockwise direction)

19 JOHN MICHAEL WRIGHT (1617–94)
George Vernon (1635/6–1702)
The builder of Sudbury. He is shown in his uniform as lieutenant-colonel of the Derbyshire militia, which guaranteed stability after the restoration of Charles II in 1660. The pose may have been influenced by Van Dyck's portrait of Strafford (a copy of which is in the Drawing Room, no. 32).

20 JOHN VANDERBANK (*c.*1694–1739)
Mary Howard, Lady Vernon (1710–40)
Signed and dated 1737
Daughter of the 6th Lord Howard of Effingham and first wife of the 1st Lord Vernon, whom she married in 1733.

21 ENOCH SEEMAN (1694–1745)
Anna Vernon, Mrs Lockwood (1710–57)
Signed and dated 1741
Sister of the 1st Lord Vernon: she married her first cousin Richard Lockwood in 1749.

22 ENOCH SEEMAN (1694–1745)
George, 1st Lord Vernon (1709–80)
Signed and dated 1740
Succeeded to Sudbury in 1718. In 1728 assumed the additional surname of Venables upon inheriting the Kinderton estates of his great-uncle, Peter Venables; created Baron Vernon of Kinderton, 1762. He is wearing a version of the Hungarian hussar uniform, which became very popular in England in the mid-eighteenth century and which was later adopted by the British Army for its hussar regiments. He installed the full-length family portraits in this room.

23 ? JOHN RILEY (1646–91)
Catherine Vernon, Mrs George Vernon (1663–1710)
Daughter of Sir Thomas Vernon of Twickenham Park, Middlesex, and third wife of George Vernon.

24 JOHN VANDERBANK (*c.*1694–1739)
*Sir William Yonge, 4th Bt (c.*1693–1755)*
He married Anne, daughter of 6th Lord Howard of Effingham, whose younger sister Mary was the 1st Lord Vernon's first wife. Vanderbank copied the pose from Kneller's portrait of the 1st Duke of Dorset at Knole.

25 MICHAEL DAHL (1656/9–1743)
Elizabeth Vernon, Lady Harcourt (1678–1748)
Daughter of Sir Thomas Vernon of Twickenham Park, Middlesex, and sister of George Vernon's third wife; married first Sir John Walter and secondly in 1724 the 1st Viscount Harcourt.

Anne Lee, who married the 1st Lord Vernon in 1741 and died only a year later; attributed to Thomas Hudson (no. 27; Saloon). She is wearing seventeenth-century fancy dress inspired by Rubens's portrait of his wife

26 THOMAS HUDSON (1701–79)
Sir William Lee, 4th Bt (1726–99)
His sister Anne (see no. 27) was the 1st Lord Vernon's
second wife. In 1763 he married Elizabeth Harcourt,
the niece of Vernon's third wife.

27 ? THOMAS HUDSON (1701–79)
Anne Lee, Lady Vernon (d.1742)
Daughter of Sir Thomas Lee, 3rd Bt; married the
1st Lord Vernon as his second wife in 1741. She is
wearing a form of fancy dress inspired by Rubens's
portrait of his wife (now in Lisbon). The drapery
may have been painted by Joseph van Aken.

28 JOHN VANDERBANK (*c*.1694–1739)
George, 1st Lord Vernon (1709–80)
Signed and dated 1736
See no. 22.

FURNITURE

The set of walnut dining-chairs, c.1735, was almost
certainly commissioned for this room by the 1st
Lord Vernon, when he inserted the full-length
family portraits. They have recently been bought
back for Sudbury with the help of the NACF.

ON MANTELPIECE:

The Louis XIV bracket clock, c.1710, with a Boulle-
work case is signed 'Gautier Paris'.

THE DRAWING ROOM

This and the adjoining room, the Library, were
made into one room by Salvin about 1853 and
redecorated in the 1920s, but the original arrangement was restored in 1969, when the rooms were
again redecorated and the dove-grey moiré wallpaper put up here. The two main reasons for this
were that Salvin had destroyed the balance of
George Vernon's plan and that the two ceilings
were very different compositions in character, and
were never intended to be seen together.

CEILING

The Drawing Room ceiling, which incorporates
the Vernon arms at each side, was put up in 1680
and is the most elaborate of all those by Bradbury
and Pettifer in the house. The motif of winged
cherubs' heads, curious to find in such a secular
setting, recalls the contemporary plasterwork of
Edward Goudge – for instance in the chapel at

A detail of Grinling Gibbons's carving of dead game in the
Drawing Room

Belton – while the whole design of the ceiling is
close to work of the 1680s at Felbrigg and Melton
Constable in Norfolk, both attributed to Goudge.
The painting in the centre of the ceiling does not
belong to the series by Laguerre and is by an
unknown artist. Whereas the Laguerres are all
painted on plaster, this is on canvas and was probably added somewhat later. It depicts *The Council of
the Gods* from Virgil's epic poem, the *Aeneid*:
Jupiter, in the centre, attempts to mediate between
his queen, Juno (with peacock), and daughter,
Venus (standing), who have been arguing over the
fate of Venus's son, Aeneas, the founder of Rome.

OVERMANTEL

The very fine carving over the chimneypiece is an
early documented work by Grinling Gibbons, an
entry in George Vernon's account book for 1678
recording a payment to him of £40 'for ye carved

Classical Ruins with Diana and Nymphs; by John Griffier the Elder (no. 29; Drawing Room)

worke on ye drawing room chimney'. Its miraculously life-like representation of dead game and fish, as well as fruit and flowers, bears comparison with Gibbons's celebrated trophies at Petworth in Sussex and at Lyme Park in Cheshire. Some restoration and rearrangement of the carving was carried out in the early nineteenth century by the cabinetmaker and dealer George Baldock. The carving was varnished in the late nineteenth century.

PICTURES

OVER DOOR:

29 JOHN GRIFFIER the Elder (1645–1718)
Classical Ruins with Diana and Nymphs
Signed: *JOHN GRIFFER*

30 JOHN HOPPNER, RA (c.1758–1810)
Georgiana Fauquier, Lady Vernon (1748–1823)
The 2nd Lord Vernon's second wife and a fearsome character, according to Horace Walpole. This portrait was sold in 1919, but later bought back by the family.

OVERMANTEL:

31 JOHN VANDERBANK (c.1694–1739)
Anne Howard, Lady Yonge (d.1775) *with a blackamoor page*
Signed and dated 1737
Daughter of the 6th Lord Howard of Effingham and wife of Sir William Yonge, 4th Bt. Her younger sister married the 1st Lord Vernon.

32 After Sir ANTHONY VAN DYCK (1599–1641)
Thomas Wentworth, 1st Earl of Strafford (1593–1641)
Lord-Deputy of Ireland. The original painting is at Petworth.

33 Attributed to GEORGE KNAPTON (1698–1778)
Lady Elizabeth Harcourt, Lady Lee (d.1811)
Daughter of the 1st Earl Harcourt and wife of Sir William Lee, 4th Bt, who were both brother-in-laws of the 1st Lord Vernon, through his second and third wives.

OVER DOOR:

34 JOHN GRIFFIER the Elder (1645–1718)
Exotic Seaport

CERAMICS

ON WALLS:

The two groups of octagonal plates are eighteenth-century Chinese *famille rose.*

CURTAINS

The festoon curtains are of a type made fashionable in the mid-eighteenth century, but known in England from engravings by Marot and available towards the end of George Vernon's lifetime. They were introduced by John Fowler in 1969.

LIGHTING

The magnificent Rococo giltwood wall-lights are about 1750.

FURNITURE

BETWEEN WINDOWS:

The pier-glass was probably made about 1740.

The longcase clock by John Bushman in a black japanned case with Chinoiserie decoration is early eighteenth-century, like the other lacquer furniture.

THE LIBRARY

This may have been the room George Vernon called 'my study'.

PLASTERWORK

The plasterwork frieze here (similar to that in the Hall) was executed by the Derby plasterer Samuel Mansfield in 1672, but the ceiling itself is close in style to Bradbury and Pettifer's work of four years later in the Long Gallery, and may well be an afterthought. Once again its keynote is the broad swirling band of acanthus foliage so favoured by Restoration architects and craftsmen.

BOOKCASES AND DECORATION

The bookcases, which may date from the end of George Vernon's lifetime or possibly from the early eighteenth century, seem to have been made for the

The Library

room, but when Salvin took down the west wall about 1853 he placed one bookcase against the west wall of the Drawing Room, where it remained until the two rooms were restored and redecorated in 1969. Then the fireplace was reopened, the chimneypiece was brought down from a bedroom, and the woodwork grained. In the seventeenth century, woodwork was seldom left in its natural state and, if not painted, was either marbled or grained.

WALLPAPER

The wallpaper was copied by Coles from a late eighteenth-century English paper, found behind one of the bookcases during the restoration of the room in 1969.

PICTURE

OVERMANTEL:

105 Style of Sir GODFREY KNELLER
(1646/9–1723)
? *Anne Pigot, Mrs Vernon* (1693–1714)
Possibly Anne Pigot, the wife of Henry Vernon (see no. 60) through whom the Venables estates devolved on the Vernon family.

CERAMICS

ON BOOKCASE SHELVES:

The Greek and Etruscan vases were discovered by the 5th Lord Vernon. William Warren Vernon in his *Recollections of Seventy-two Years* wrote: 'during this summer [1843] my father carried out extensive excavations among the tombs of Cumae, and made a very beautiful collection of Etruscan and Greek vases which are now at Sudbury.'

SCULPTURE

ON TOP OF BOOKCASES:

Eighteenth-century plaster busts of men of letters and classical thinkers, including Alexander Pope and John Locke (nearest the fireplace, to left and right), and Francis Bacon. They were a common feature of country-house libraries.

From the Library, visitors return through the Entrance Passage, and turn right into the Stone Passage.

THE STONE PASSAGE

This corridor links the servants' quarters in the east wing with the family rooms in the main house. A framed genealogy of the Vernon family hangs to the left of the door to Lady Vernon's Sitting Room.

PICTURES

35 ENGLISH, c.1750–1800
Sudbury from the South: Evening
By the same hand as nos. 36 and 37.

37 ENGLISH, c.1750–1800
Sudbury from the North: Morning

36 ENGLISH, c.1750–1800
Sudbury seen from the Lake
Painted after the original balustrade on the roof of the house had disappeared, the steps to the porch had been altered and George Vernon's formal garden had been replaced by a landscape setting.

37a ENGLISH, c.1750–1800
Sudbury from the North

112 ENGLISH, nineteenth-century
A Bay Thoroughbred, Trustee

97 ENGLISH, early nineteenth-century
A Grey Horse

LORD VERNON'S STUDY

This small comfortable room was used by the present baron's father for business. It is hung with estate maps of various dates, including one dated 1794 by Samuel Botham.

PICTURE

103 FRANK CADOGAN COWPER (1877–1958)
Violet Clay, Lady Vernon (1895–1978)
Wife of the 9th Lord Vernon and mother of the late baron.

FURNITURE

The openwork, or 'skeleton', clock is mid-nineteenth-century, English.

Through the door is Lady Vernon's Sitting Room.

LADY VERNON'S SITTING ROOM

Decorated in the cool sage green that is redolent of the 1930s, when this room was last in everyday use, by Violet, Lady Vernon (1895–1978).

*Lady Vernon's
Sitting Room*

PICTURES

OVERMANTEL:

CHARLES PHILLIPS (1708–47)
The Warren Family
Signed and dated 1734
Borlase Warren and his wife, Ann Harpur, are
seated on the right. Through a later connection
with the Warren family, the Vernons of Sudbury
inherited great estates, mills and mines at Poynton
in Cheshire.

111 ENGLISH, late seventeenth-century
Member of the Vernon Family

46 ? WILLIAM HOARE (1707–92)
Unidentified Lady
Pastel

THOMAS GAINSBOROUGH (1727–88)
Louisa Barbara Mansel, Lady Vernon (1732–86)
First wife to the 2nd Lord Vernon.

52 ENGLISH, eighteenth-century
Unidentified Lady
Pastel
The frames of this and no. 46 are fine examples in
the style of William Kent.

ON RIGHT-HAND WALL:

VIOLET, LADY VERNON (1895–1978) and RALPH
SHIRLEY
Lady Vernon's Sitting Room
It shows the room as it was in the 1930s.

SCULPTURE

DAVID WILLIAMS-ELLIS (b.1959)
John, 10th Lord Vernon (1923–2000)
A bronze bust commissioned in 1988 by the National
Trust's Foundation for Art of the late Lord Vernon,
whose daughter continues to live on the estate.

THE SMALL DINING ROOM

Across the corridor is the Small Dining Room, hung
with family portraits and furnished much as it must
have been when the room was created late in the
eighteenth or early in the nineteenth century. Originally the room (also known as the Oak Parlour)
filled the entire space of the Stone Passage as well as
the Small Dining Room, mirroring the form and
area of the Great Hall opposite.

*The Small
Dining Room*

PICTURES

41 JOHN LUCAS (1807–74)
Isabella Ellison, Lady Vernon (1805–53)
First wife of the 5th Lord Vernon.

40 After MARK OATES (*c.*1750–after 1821)
Admiral Sir John Borlase Warren (1753–1822)
Father of Frances Maria Warren, wife of the 4th
Lord Vernon; fought in the Napoleonic Wars and
was later ambassador extraordinary and pleni-
potentiary to Russia after the Peace of Amiens in
1802, when he may have been given the candlestand in the Great Hall.

39 JOHN COLLIER (1850–1934)
George John, 5th Lord Vernon (1803–66)
Signed. Painted in 1908 from a photograph taken
in 1859
On the death of his mother in 1837, when he in-
herited the Poynton estates, he assumed the name of
Warren. A well-known student of Dante, he was
responsible for forming the library at Sudbury.

99 T. MAZZONI
William Warren Vernon (1834–1919)
Oval. Signed and dated 1874
Younger son of the 5th Lord Vernon.

100 Attributed to JOHN HOPPNER (*c.*1758–1810)
George Venables Vernon, 2nd Baron Vernon
(1735–1813)
Succeeded to Sudbury in 1780.

CERAMICS

A Chelsea-Derby dessert service (1770–84).

*On leaving the Small Dining Room, descend the stone
stairs in the Butler's Pantry to reach the basement.*

THE BILLIARD ROOM

Billiard-rooms became fashionable additions to
country houses in the early nineteenth century, and
a billiard-table was installed by Salvin in the Great
Hall, probably in the 1830s. In the early 1870s Devey
devised a scheme for a billiard-room in the basement, which seems never to have been completed.

The present ornate ceiling, balustrade and lava-
tories were probably inserted at the turn of the
century by Romaine-Walker. The Victorian chan-
delier was moved here from the Queen's Room by
the National Trust.

THE KITCHEN

Until about 1872 this room was partitioned into the
housekeeper's storeroom, a knife-cleaning room
and boot room. During the major building works
of the 1870s it became the still-room, where the
housekeeper would prepare and store pickles, jams
and jellies. The oak fitted cupboards were probably
put in at this time.

It became the main kitchen in 1922, when the 9th
Lord Vernon returned to living at Sudbury and
required a kitchen closer to the Small Dining Room
immediately above.

The blue cotton housekeeper's apron was a gift
from Mrs Marion Kent and was used by her while
in service at Sudbury.

THE OAK STAIRCASE

The visitor now ascends the Oak Staircase, which
was reconstructed by George Devey between 1873
and 1883, though reusing some of the balusters and
newels from the original secondary stairs. The visitor then passes further suites of family rooms at
mezzanine level, to the Long Gallery above.

PICTURE

38 ENGLISH, *c.*1820
Frances Maria Warren, Lady Vernon (1784–1837)
The wife of the 4th Lord Vernon. She brought the
Poynton estates in Cheshire into the family.

FURNITURE

Mid-eighteenth-century longcase clock by Joseph Kirk
of Nottingham.

THE LONG GALLERY

It is most unusual to find a Long Gallery in a Charles
II house and its existence is one of the most puzzl-
ing, as well as one of the most magnificent, features
of Sudbury. The room, just over 138 feet in length,
was completed about 1676, for in November of that
year Bradbury was paid £101 2s for the ceiling,
perhaps the finest of its kind in any English house.
George Vernon was immensely proud of the Nor-
man origins of his family, and it is at least possible
that he conceived the Long Gallery as a consciously

The Long Gallery

old-fashioned gesture – a way of stressing the antiquity of the Vernons, with family portraits on the walls running parallel with the busts of Roman emperors in the frieze above, and with the shields in the ceiling perhaps originally intended to be painted with the quarterings of his ancestors' marriage alliances. It has recently been suggested that the emperors are caricatures of contemporary notables, including Charles II and James II.

CEILING PLASTERWORK

The detail of Bradbury and Pettifer's plasterwork is endlessly rewarding, from the almost caricature heads of the emperors themselves, and the sculptural quality of the shells and palm fronds between, to the delicate curling seed-pods of the ubiquitous acanthus, and the sheer playfulness of the grasshoppers, dancing round the rosette in the ceiling above the central bay window.

PANELLING AND FLOOR

By comparison, the panelling is of very simple design. It was last painted in 1864 by the London decorators Howard & Sons, who also installed the raised floor in the central bay on the south. The rest of the floor, of oak from the estate, was renewed by Salvin in 1851 and was kept highly polished until 1967.

The ceiling was repainted to tone in with the walls during the restoration of 1969–70. During the later nineteenth century the Gallery appears to have been the room most used by the family. The walls on all sides were lined with polished pine bookcases, containing the bulk of the 5th Lord Vernon's huge library. It remained thus until 1967.

PICTURES

The Long Gallery is hung with conventional seventeenth-century portraits, which have probably always been here, mostly representing members of George Vernon's family. Some of them (like those of the Shirleys) have splendid seventeenth-century 'Sunderland' frames, recognisable by their 'auricular', or ear-like, ornament. The best are perhaps those by John Michael Wright, the most important native-born painter in Restoration England. Wright's unflinching style gives his work a vivacity rare for the period, but cost him clients, and he died in relative poverty.

80 ENGLISH, seventeenth-century
Unidentified Lady, formerly known as Mary Hawtrey, Lady Bankes
This cannot be the same sitter as no. 55; it may be one of her relations.

79 After JOHN MICHAEL WRIGHT (1617–94)
Elizabeth Washington, Countess Ferrers (d.1693)
First wife of Sir Robert Shirley, later Lord Ferrers, to whom she bore seventeen children.

55 ENGLISH, mid-seventeenth-century
Lady called Lady Bankes
Daughter of Ralph Hawtrey and wife of Lord Chief Justice Bankes. She defended Corfe Castle in Dorset during two sieges by Parliamentary troops; on the second occasion it fell as a result of treachery.

81 Sir GODFREY KNELLER (1646/9–1723)
Dorothy Shirley, Mrs Vernon (d.1680)
Sister of Robert, Earl Ferrers, and second wife of George Vernon.

92 JOHN MICHAEL WRIGHT (1617–94)
Margaret Onley, Mrs Vernon (1642–75)
Oval
Dated on the reverse 1660, the year she married George Vernon as his first wife (see no. 75)
It is one of a series of oval portraits of the family by Wright, for which Vernon paid in 1659/60.

77 JOHN MICHAEL WRIGHT (1617–94)
Mrs Onley
Mother of Margaret Onley, George Vernon's first wife.

76 JOHN MICHAEL WRIGHT (1617–94)
Sir Robert Shirley, 7th Bt and 1st Earl Ferrers (1650–1717)
Steward to the Royal household, 1685–1705.

75 JOHN MICHAEL WRIGHT (1617–94)
Margaret Onley, Mrs Vernon (1642–75)
First wife of George Vernon.

83 SIMON DUBOIS (1632–1708)
'A Son of Sir Thomas Vernon' (later inscription on portrait)
Painted oval
Signed and dated 1682

74 ?DUTCH, seventeenth- to eighteenth-century
Figures by a Fountain

85 ENGLISH, mid-eighteenth-century
Unknown Officer
Possibly an early oil painting by Francis Cotes (1726–70).

73 ENGLISH, late seventeenth-century
Reputedly Mrs Wright and Child
Possibly Henry Vernon's second wife, Matilda Wright, as a child, with her mother, who was the wife of Thomas Wright of Longstone, Derby.

72 Style of Sir ANTHONY VAN DYCK (1599–1641)
Sir Robert Shirley, 4th Bt (1629–56)
Husband of Catherine Okeover and father of Dorothy, second wife of George Vernon. He was

Margaret Onley (1642–75), George Vernon's first wife; by J. M. Wright (no. 75; Long Gallery)

committed by Cromwell to the Tower, where he died.

71 ? JOHN RILEY (1646–91)
Anne, Lady Vernon (d.1702)
Wife of Sir Thomas Vernon (no. 88) and mother-in-law of George Vernon.

84 JOHN MICHAEL WRIGHT (1617–94)
'Colonel Vernon'
Oval
Inscribed with his name and possibly of Edward Vernon, uncle of George, builder of the house.

87 After WILLIAM SHEPPARD (active *c.*1640–65)
Thomas Killigrew (1612–83)
Playwright and royal favourite, and in 1660 groom of the bedchamber. The original portrait was painted in Venice in 1650.

70 ? JOHN RILEY (1646–91)
Miss Vernon, Mrs Took
Sister of Sir Thomas Vernon and aunt of George Vernon's third wife, Catherine.

69 Style of Sir ANTHONY VAN DYCK (1599–1641)
Sir Charles Shirley, 3rd Bt (1623–46)
Elder brother of Sir Robert Shirley, and so uncle by marriage of George Vernon.

68 Style of Sir PETER LELY (1618–80)
Barbara Villiers, Duchess of Cleveland (*c.*1641–1709)
Mistress of Charles II.

88 ? JOHN RILEY (1646–91)
Sir Thomas Vernon (d.1710)
A London merchant, one of whose fifteen children, Catherine, was the third wife of George Vernon. He is buried in Sudbury church. Companion to no. 71.

67 ? DUTCH, seventeenth- to eighteenth-century
Shepherd and Shepherdess in a Landscape

89 ENGLISH, eighteenth-century
Unidentified Lady

66 ENGLISH, seventeenth-century
Henry Vernon (1686–1719) *as a Boy*
See no. 60 (Great Staircase Landing).

65 After Sir PETER LELY (1618–80)
Nell Gwyn (1650–87)
Actress and mistress of Charles II.

64 Style of Sir ANTHONY VAN DYCK (1599–1641)
Catherine Okeover, Lady Shirley (d.1672)
Wife of Sir Robert Shirley, 4th Bt, whose daughter Dorothy was George Vernon's second wife.

63 ENGLISH, eighteenth-century
Henry Vernon (1686–1719)
See no. 60 (Great Staircase Landing).

62 ? Sir GODFREY KNELLER (1646/9–1723)
Louise de Kéroualle, Duchess of Portsmouth (1649–1734)
Accompanied Henrietta, sister of Charles II, to England as her maid of honour in 1670, soon afterwards becoming the King's mistress.

91 ENGLISH, *c.*1760–70
Unidentified Man

93 Sir GODFREY KNELLER (1646/9–1723)
'Captain Vernon'
The portrait is inscribed with his name.

90 JOHN MICHAEL WRIGHT (1617–94)
George Vernon (1635/6–1702)
Oval

61 JOHN MICHAEL WRIGHT (1617–94)
Edward Onley
Father of Margaret Onley, George Vernon's first wife.

LIGHTING

The early Georgian-style giltwood chandeliers were made in the 1920s by Lenygon & Morant, a firm specialising in interior decoration for historic houses.

A late seventeenth- or early eighteenth-century gesso side-table in the Long Gallery

FURNITURE

The walnut chairs and sofas upholstered in modern blue fabric are early eighteenth-century.

The gesso side-tables with veined red and grey marble tops are of an unusual late seventeenth- or early eighteenth-century design.

The pair of eagle console tables with grey marble tops is about 1740.

The library table decorated with floral marquetry is nineteenth-century. Beside it is a late seventeenth-century rosewood burgomaster's chair.

SCULPTURE

ON SIDE-TABLES:

The bronzes, of *Nessus abducting Deianeira* and of *A Roman abducting a Sabine Woman*, are French, late seventeenth-century, imitating the style of Giambologna (1529–1608); they are mounted on contemporary French stands.

THE TALBOT ROOM

The room may take its name from an ancestor of George Vernon, who married Anne Talbot, daughter of the 2nd Earl of Shrewsbury. It was used as a bedroom, with a small staircase to the attic floor, until the 1880s, when Theodosius Coxon, the clerk of works, transformed it into a galleried library to take the overflow of books from the Long Gallery. The cast-iron spiral staircase was made at that time by Hayward Bros & Eckstein of London.

SCULPTURE

A bronze bust of Dante has been added to this room as a memorial to the 5th Lord Vernon, who was a leading scholar of the Italian poet and collected most of the books once shelved here. It is by the Neapolitan sculptor Sabatino de Angelis (b.1838), who also cast some of Alfred Gilbert's best bronzes.

FURNITURE

The ebonised and walnut folio stand is c.1825.

The mid-Georgian 'metamorphic' library steps convert into a leather-topped stool.

THE GREAT STAIRCASE LANDING

The two great doorcases at the top of the Staircase, leading to the Queen's Room and the Dante Room, were carved by Edward Pierce in 1676–7, at the same time as his work on the balustrade.

PICTURES

53 LOUIS LAGUERRE (1663–1721)
Alexander attacking a Scythian (?) City
Mural. Signed

18 Studio of Sir PETER LELY (1618–80)
Barbara Villiers, Duchess of Cleveland (c.1641–1709)
Mistress of Charles II.

56 ENGLISH, 1624
Sir Arnold Warren

108 WILLIAM HAMILTON (1751–1801)
King Edgar's First Interview with Queen Elfrida
Painted in 1744
Not part of the Vernon collection, but a bequest from Vera and Aileen Woodroffe through the NACF. It is, however, doubly apt at Sudbury, both as another very early example of a depiction of British history (see no. 54), and because the interview between King Edgar and his future second wife, Queen Aelfryth or Elfrida, apparently took place at Corfe Castle, where she was later to have his son and her stepson, King Edward the Martyr, assassinated in order to put her own son, Ethelred the Unready, on the throne (AD 978). Corfe Castle was later to be bought by Sir John Bankes (no. 78), an ancestor of Frances Warren, Lady Vernon (no. 38).

57 ENGLISH, seventeenth-century
Supposed portrait of Sir William Borlase, Kt (d.1630)
Father of Sir John Borlase, 1st Bt. The armour suggests an earlier sitter.

86 ? THOMAS MURRAY (1663–1735)
? Henry Vernon (1686–1719)
Oval
See no. 60 (Great Staircase Landing).

58 ? MICHAEL DAHL (1656/9–1743)
Thomas, 1st Lord Mansel (1688–1723)
Comptroller of the Household to Queen Anne; created Lord Mansel, 1711/12. The 4th Lord Mansel's daughter married the 2nd Lord Vernon.

The Talbot Room

59 ? ENGLISH, late seventeenth-century
Women sacrificing to Janus
The herm has two faces and presumably represents Janus Bifrons, the God of the year and gardens, and the intercessor through whom prayers reached the immortals. He was worshipped by the Romans and was thought to have introduced a Golden Age.

60 ENGLISH, *c*.1715
Henry Vernon (1686–1719)
Son of George Vernon; married first Anne Pigot, through whom the Vernon family inherited the Kinderton estates and assumed the additional name of Venables; and secondly Matilda Wright. By his first wife he was the father of the 1st Lord Vernon.

48 ? GERARD SOEST (*c*.1600–81)
? *Alice Bankes, Lady Borlase (1621–83)*
Eldest daughter of Sir John Bankes, married Sir John Borlase in 1637. Shows her as an older woman than in Van Dyck's portrait at Kingston Lacy.

OVERMANTEL:

49 HENDRIK DANCKERTS (*c*.1625–79)
Figures in a Classical Garden

50 Studio of Sir ANTHONY VAN DYCK (1599–1641)
Sir John Borlase, 1st Bt (1619–72)
Created a baronet 1642. The original portrait is at Kingston Lacy.

THE QUEEN'S ROOM

Known as the Great Stairhead Chamber when the house was first built, it owes its present name to Queen Adelaide, the consort of William IV, who leased Sudbury for three years in 1840, during her widowhood. It was one of the first rooms to be finished by George Vernon and was completed before he had come into contact with the London craftsmen. The ceiling is by Samuel Mansfield and the alabaster chimneypiece and overmantel were carved by William Wilson in 1670. Coxon put up the mouldings round the doors in the late nineteenth century, having discovered them in storage. When the room was restored in 1969, it was discovered that the section of the cornice above the overmantel was of alabaster and part of Wilson's design. The silk wall-hangings have been copied from the eighteenth-century fabric previously in the room.

PICTURES

Beside the bed hangs a print of Queen Adelaide and in the frame beneath a moving document – instructions for her funeral which the Queen Dowager wrote at Sudbury in November 1841.

47 ITALIAN, seventeenth-century
Flowers and Fruit
Presumably a copy of no. 51.

78 GILBERT JACKSON (active 1622–40)
Sir John Bankes, Lord Chief Justice (1589–1644)
Attorney-general, 1634; chief justice, 1641. The original portrait is at Kingston Lacy in Dorset.

The alabaster overmantel in the Queen's Room was carved by William Wilson

Adam and Eve; from the Frans Francken cabinet in the Queen's Room

OVER DOOR:

51 ITALIAN, seventeenth-century
Flowers and Fruit

FURNITURE

The bed cornice is mid-eighteenth-century but the bed itself has been altered.

The seventeenth-century Flemish ebony cabinet, which is on a later stand, has panels of biblical subjects painted on copper by Frans Francken the Younger (1581–1642).

The rest of the furniture is eighteenth-century; it includes a Dutch Neo-classical wardrobe, a pair of mahogany tables and, above a mahogany serpentine chest-of-drawers, a fine gilt pier-glass made about 1740.

ON CHEST-OF-DRAWERS:

The large stumpwork box on the chest-of-drawers bears the date 1671 (or possibly 1672), and the name of its owner 'Hannah Trapham' engraved on the lock.

CERAMICS

Oriental blue-and-white vases.

Late seventeenth-century English Delftware blue-dash charger, decorated with William of Orange on horseback, crudely overpainted to transform the King into a bishop.

English Delftware blue-dash charger decorated with tulips.

PICTURE

IN PASSAGE BETWEEN QUEEN'S ROOM AND PORCH ROOM:

116 HUGH BUCHANAN (b.1958)
Sudbury Hall, Derbyshire
The reflection in the Drawing Room pier-glass is depicted in this early commission by the Foundation for Art and purchased for Sudbury in 1985.

THE PORCH ROOM

This room was originally the dressing-room attached to the State Bedroom (now the Queen's Room). It is arranged so that visitors may read or rest at the end of their tour of the house. The wallpaper was hand-printed by Coles and put up in 1969.

PICTURES

It is hung with prints, mainly recording the naval exploits of Admiral Vernon and his contemporaries in the early eighteenth century.

FIREPLACE

The tiles in the fireplace are Liverpool Delftware of about 1770, and the chimneypiece itself was concocted by Coxon in the 1890s. It incorporates fragments of seventeenth-century carving, including a bedhead 'which has lain in wood yard a number of years' and 'figures bought at Uttoxeter'.

The castellated building seen from the window is the Gothick deercote, one of the most elaborate in the country. Though basically eighteenth-century in date, it was radically altered in the nineteenth. The painting in the Stone Passage below shows it as being painted white, without the present red-brick 'gatehouse' at the centre.

THE VELVET BEDROOM

This is possibly the room referred to by George Vernon as the 'Gallery Chamber'. Its present form dates from Anthony Salvin's work at Sudbury in the early 1850s. The room is not furnished, as it is used occasionally for exhibitions.

THE FIRST-FLOOR CORRIDOR

PICTURES

45 ENGLISH, eighteenth-century
Unidentified Lady

42 W. E. MILLER (active 1873–1903)
Diana Vernon, Mrs Newton (1852–1929)
Eldest daughter of the 6th Lord Vernon and wife of Charles Newton.

43 GEORGE RICHMOND, RA (1809–96)
Augustus Henry, 6th Lord Vernon (1829–83), 1866
See no. 10.

44 JAMES SWINTON (1816–88)
Lady Harriet Anson, Lady Vernon (1827–98), 1849
Third daughter of the 1st Earl of Lichfield; married in 1851 6th Lord Vernon.

95 W. E. MILLER (active 1873–1903)
Caroline Maria Vernon, Mrs Anson (1826–1918), 1881
Eldest child of 5th Lord Vernon and wife of Canon Frederick Anson.

96 W. E. MILLER (active 1873–1903)
Canon Frederick Anson, 1881
Rector of Sudbury and subsequently Canon of Windsor.

82 ENGLISH, eighteenth-century
? Margaret Molyneux, Mrs Warren
Daughter of Sir Richard Molyneux of Sefton and wife of John Warren of Poynton (no. 94).

94 ENGLISH, eighteenth-century
? John Warren (c.1535–88)
Second son of Sir Edward Warren of Poynton, Cheshire; married Margaret, daughter of Sir Richard Molyneux (no. 82). The family descended from a bastard son of the last Warenne Earl of Surrey; in 1826 the Poynton estates passed to the Vernons by marriage. Although dated 1580, painted in the eighteenth century.

THE GARDEN AND CHURCH

The surroundings of Sudbury have changed more radically and more often than the house itself. John Griffier's *c.*1690 painting (illustrated on p. 37) shows that George Vernon laid out a walled garden typical of the Restoration period, which was centred on the south front of the house. It was divided into grass parterres by gravel paths, which were ornamented by statues on plinths. Beyond the walls were orchards with a formal grid of avenues, while a flight of broad steps led down to rectangular fish-ponds.

Very few features of George Vernon's original formal layout can now be traced, as in the mid-eighteenth century his grandson, the 1st Lord Vernon, 'naturalised' the landscape in the manner of 'Capability' Brown. He swept away the walled garden, formed a serpentine lake out of the fish-ponds, reduced the old avenues to clumps of trees, and built the Gothick deercote in the park to the north. The two lodges in front of the house were designed by Thomas Gardner of Uttoxeter in 1787.

A view of Sudbury from the north in the late eighteenth century, showing the deercote on the left (no. 37; Stone Passage)

The 4th Lord Vernon, who inherited in 1829, was a keen agriculturalist inspired by the example of Coke of Norfolk and the writings of Arthur Young. He took the process of naturalisation still further by draining the lake and trying to grow maize on it – binding the works of the radical essayist William Cobbett in paper made from the crop. He also called in the landscape gardener W. S. Gilpin, the nephew and pupil of the great advocate of the Picturesque, William Gilpin, but little seems to have been done before Lord Vernon's death in 1835.

In the late 1830s George, 5th Lord Vernon, who was steeped in the culture of his beloved Italy, embarked on wholesale changes to the garden with the advice of his cousin, Vice-Admiral Octavius Vernon-Harcourt. Following the younger Gilpin's plans, he aimed to enhance the Picturesque qualities of the landscape – refilling and enlarging the lake for instance, creating the island opposite the house, and providing serpentine walks through the shrub-

beries towards its western end. But he also turned to the head gardener at Chatsworth, Joseph Paxton, who belonged to a new generation of designers that advocated a return to greater formality with lavish schemes of bedding-out. So Lord Vernon constructed two wide terraces, with formal flower-beds, on the south side of the house. Salvin came up with sketches for grand new gates on to the turn-pike road to the north of the house, but these do not seem to have been built.

Gilpin introduced Lord Vernon to his brother-in-law, William Andrews Nesfield, who submitted seven pages of 'General Observations & Remedial Propositions' in September 1852. Nesfield was highly critical of what he found, considering 'neither the design nor the quality of the details are after the manner of "the olden time", but modern and non-descript'. He produced an Italianate scheme for elaborate *broderie* parterres along the terraces and on the island, but money seems to have been running short, and so far as is known no work was carried

Sudbury from across the lake in the 1860s

The footbridge was built in the early nineteenth century as an eye-catcher at the east end of the lake

out. In 1919 and 1924–5 William Baron & Sons made further changes to the grounds for the 9th Lord Vernon.

In 1970 the National Trust made two star-shaped borders on the top terrace and planted the other terraces and paths with topiary plants. At the same time a quincunx of limes (so called after the repeating pattern of trees grouped in fives) was planted on the lawn in front of the nineteenth-century wing.

THE CHURCH

The church of All Saints appears to the west of the house in John Griffier's painting and has always had close links with the estate and with the Vernon family. In 1873–7, 1881 and 1883 it was comprehensively restored for the 6th Lord Vernon by George Devey. He raised the tower and added the pinnacles, replaced some of the windows in the Perpendicular style, and reroofed the whole building. Inside, he replaced the north transept with a second north aisle, removed the gallery and installed new pews.

The Vernon chapel contains a fine series of family monuments. The most important are: an alabaster tomb-chest to John Vernon (d.1600) and his wife Mary, who lies below him; in the centre, an urn on a free-standing plinth to George Vernon's first wife, Margaret (d.1675), by Edward Pierce; a wall-tablet to George Vernon (d.1702) by Edward Stanton; and profile portraits of the 4th Lord Vernon (d.1835) and his wife Frances (d.1837) between Grecian twin stelae, by John Francis. By the door there is also a charming low-relief marble tondo commemorating two young children of the 6th Lord Vernon.

The stained glass includes a memorial window of 1885 to the 6th Lord Vernon by Burlison & Grylls.

SUDBURY AND THE VERNONS

THE DERBYSHIRE VERNONS

Derbyshire may lack an ancient cathedral, but it is extraordinarily rich in great country houses, from Hardwick, Bolsover and Chatsworth, to Calke, Melbourne and Kedleston. Two of the finest were built by the Vernons, who have been among the leading Derbyshire families for at least seven centuries: Haddon, amid the peaks in the north-west of the county; and Sudbury, 20 miles to the south, in the gentler country bordering Staffordshire.

Haddon Hall, the perfect castle on a hill of the English imagination, had been the home of Vernons since the twelfth century. When it passed to Sir Richard Vernon in 1515, his younger brother John had to strike out on his own. He did this in the traditional way by marrying a local heiress, Helen Montgomery of Cubley, from whom he inherited the Sudbury estate in 1513. By a succession of such judicious marriages, often with relatives, John Vernon's descendants protected and expanded their Sudbury domain.

John's son Henry was brought up in the old parsonage at Sudbury (there was not yet a manor house), probably with his cousin, George, 'the King of the Peak' and the last of the Haddon Vernons. However, he chose to live, not at Sudbury, but in north Derbyshire at Hazelbadge Hall, which he rebuilt in 1549. Henry spread his influence into neighbouring Staffordshire by marrying Margaret Swinnerton of Swinnerton and Hilton in 1547. With George Vernon's help, he consolidated his position within Derbyshire seven years later, when he became a county MP and knight of the shire. Henry Vernon was a proud man, who was fined in 1555 for attending the local assizes (where he was a JP) with an excessively ostentatious retinue of liveried retainers. But he also seems to have been a learned one, dividing his library between his two sons, John and Henry, on his death in 1569.

John Vernon, as the elder, inherited Sudbury;

Henry received the Staffordshire estate of Hilton. All seems to have been well between the brothers until Henry decided to marry Dorothy Heveningham. A remarkable poem by John Harestaffe, who was steward to John Vernon from 1591, describes the bitter family dispute that followed:

Yong Henryes match did verie much displease
His [bachelor] elder brother John, who for to raise
Their house and name did formerlie intend,
That all his lands should after him discend
On Henry. But that marriage chang'd his mynd
Soe much that afterwards he was unkynd
Both to his brother's Infant, and his wyffe,
Soe that amongst theim soon befell great styffe
And suites in lawe.

Henry died in 1592, and perhaps to prevent the family estates falling into Dorothy's hands, John Vernon, by then in his forties and still a bachelor, decided to marry Mary Littleton, the recent widow of his cousin Walter Vernon of Houndshill and – most importantly – the mother of a son, Edward, bearing the Vernon name. For when John was laid to rest eight years later in a magnificent alabaster wall-tomb in Sudbury church, he had still not produced an heir of his own. Battle was now joined in earnest between John and Henry's widows. Harestaffe sided with Mary Vernon, 'ever of a vertuous mynd, constant to truth, to frends and children kynd', against 'the yong and loftie Dame', Dorothy. Mary took her case to London, where she petitioned the King's first minister, Sir Robert Cecil:

Then she by Harestaffe quickly was directed,
To knowe this greate man by his stature small,
And by his entringe in ye first of all.

Dorothy encouraged her nephew Francis Buck to resort to mob violence against Mary:

    . . . he came againe to Sudburie,

Where havinge gather'd much lewde companie,
Gainst whom she nere comitted anie fault
With open force they did her House assault.
… The Revelles then began: They make good cheare,
They found ye house well stor'd with bread & beare,
Beef, mutton, bacon, all things els besyde,
Which good housekeepers use for to provyde;
They frolick with their frendes, & make noe spare,
But lash out that for which they nere took care.

The quarrel was finally ended in the time-honoured Tudor fashion by marrying Mary's son Edward to Dorothy's daughter Margaret in 1613. Mary Vernon handed over the Sudbury estate to the young couple, and before her death in 1622 built them a new house, as Edward gratefully acknowledged on her monument in the church: 'Such was her charitie and vertuous mind she built a mannor house at Sudbury.' Harestaffe confirms this:

And where noe Mannor house was on ye ground,
She built one newe which cost her many a pounde.

The tomb of John and Mary Vernon in Sudbury church

Edward and Margaret also built new walls in the garden: the doorway into the churchyard is carved with their initials and the date 1626.

Like his father and grandfather, Henry Vernon (1615–60) married a Vernon heiress – Muriel Vernon, the daughter of Sir George Vernon of Haslington in Cheshire. He seems not to have got on with his father, and perhaps for this reason preferred to live on his wife's Cheshire estates. Vernon clung on to his inheritance through the Civil War 'with much payne and Trouble', as his tomb acknowledges. He sided with Parliament and raised 300 men for the cause in Cheshire. The Royalists promptly imprisoned him and indicted him for high treason. Despite this, Vernon was accused of consorting with the enemy by Parliament, which fined him and threatened to confiscate his estate. He came through these turmoils unscathed, but died in March 1660 aged only 45 on the eve of a new era for the country and for Sudbury.

GEORGE VERNON AND THE BUILDING OF THE HOUSE

Henry Vernon's son George was about 25 when he inherited the Sudbury estate, which was then worth at least £3,000 per annum. In 1662 he was described as 'a prudent young man, sober and active, … near allied to most of the gentry and nobility of Staffordshire, Derbyshire, Shropshire and Cheshire'. He had secured another lucrative alliance around 1660 by marrying Margaret Onley, an heiress from Catesby in Northamptonshire. During his 42 years as squire of Sudbury, he held numerous positions within the county, serving as High Sheriff in 1663–4, and MP for Derby in 1679–81 and 1698–1700. Fearful of the country descending again into the civil war that had almost destroyed his father, he loudly opposed the Catholic Duke of York succeeding Charles II as King: he thought it 'disgustful to the country in general to obey any orders or to act under any Roman Catholic'.

A man of George Vernon's energy, wealth, political ambition and social position would hardly have been content with his grandmother's modest manor house, and he seems to have set about building the present Sudbury Hall on a new site soon

George Vernon (1635/6–1702), the builder of the house; by J. M. Wright (no. 19; Saloon)

after succeeding. (A survey he had made of the estate in 1659 apparently shows that the old house stood further to the west and that he demolished it.) In 1661–2 he was buying bricks – more than 1,200,000 in all – mainly from Sudbury Park and the Oak's Green area. For the rest of his life he was active either constructing or decorating his new house, laying out the garden (see p. 31) or improving the village and estate.

Although Sudbury was intended for the 'politer way of living' that the Restoration introduced (according to the diarist John Evelyn), it looked back stylistically to the Jacobean era. For by 1660 Derbyshire was somewhat isolated from the latest architectural trends. In the late sixteenth and early seventeenth centuries Robert Smythson and his son John had designed a series of splendid buildings in the region, among them Wollaton Hall, Hardwick and Bolsover, but there seems to have been no one to carry on the tradition after John's death in 1634, although both his son Huntingdon and his grandson

John were architects. However, their influence continued, as can be seen in the County Hall in Derby built in 1659, and there are certain resemblances between that building, the Chapel at Locko Park (consecrated in 1673), the windows of William Sacheverell's house in Derby (as recorded in a painting at Renishaw Hall), the remodelling of Longford Hall, and Sudbury. The style of the County Hall and Locko Chapel is conservative, as one might expect in a county where neither Inigo Jones nor John Webb made any contribution, and it is worth remarking that when George Vernon was planning his house in about 1660, the key Charles II works – Clarendon House, London, and Eltham Lodge, Kent – had not yet been started. Thus it is not surprising that there are many aspects of the house that strike us as Jacobean.

The E-shape with a rich central frontispiece is an old-fashioned idea in the 1660s and so are the diapered brickwork and the nine- and twelve-light stone mullioned-and-transomed windows (the diapered brickwork may, however, be an allusion to the fret of the Vernon coat of arms). Details like the base panels to the Doric columns of the frontispiece with their round and diamond-shaped brooches, the panels over the ground-floor windows, and the hesitant triglyphs and the metopes of the frieze on the garden front, might all be dated before 1620, if found on a house nearer London, but the brooches occur at the County Hall and Locko.

The internal planning of the house is also decidedly old-fashioned. The Entrance Passage divides the house in two like a medieval screens passage, with the Great Hall, principal rooms and staircase to the west, and the kitchen, domestic offices and smaller family rooms to the east – very much the traditional arrangement. On the first floor the Great Staircase, Great Chamber (now the Queen's Room) and Long Gallery are placed in much the same positions as in the Elizabethan Hardwick Hall. The Long Gallery is also a somewhat anachronistic feature to find in a house of the 1660s. Perhaps Vernon was seeking to rival the Long Gallery in the Vernons' former Derbyshire seat at Haddon or that at Hardwick. Much subterfuge with blind windows and false floors was required to make the symmetrical exterior accord with the unsymmetrical interior.

Sudbury from the south, showing the original formal garden around George Vernon's house; by John Griffier the Elder, c.1690 (no. 1; Entrance Passage)

However, there are progressive aspects to the design. The hipped roof and the central cupola are almost hallmarks of the Charles II domestic style, and if the proportions of this part of the design have been altered by the loss of the original balustrade crowning the roof and its replacement by a stone balustrading rising above the main cornice, the fault is not George Vernon's. The massive chimneystacks may be Jacobean in scale, but their treatment suggests knowledge of those at Clarendon House. The carving in the pediments of both frontispieces is also typical of the Charles II period. But there is no domestic precedent for the tracery windows by which George Vernon evidently set such store: they might be traced back to the more Gothic work of Robert Smythson at Wollaton Hall in Nottinghamshire, but possibly these were a local fashion, for similar ones existed at the Derby home of William Sacheverell, one

of Vernon's political adversaries, with whom he was later reconciled.

George Vernon kept accounts of all he spent on building and decorating his house from 1659 until 1701, and consequently we have an unusually complete picture of its progress. No architect is mentioned, and so we must presume that he designed the house himself. This would not be as unusual then as it seems today, for a gentleman was expected to have knowledge of building and surveying, and there was some suspicion of the then very new profession of architect. Roger North, who was a contemporary, wrote that he preferred to make his own designs, because 'a profest architect is proud, opinionative and troublesome, seldome at hand, and a head workman pretending to ye designing part, is full of paultry vulgar contrivances; therefore be your owne architect, or sitt still'. The accounts show that Vernon also took a close interest in buying all the various building materials for Sudbury.

The only seventeenth-century architectural drawing to survive at Sudbury – a plan of the staircase – is annotated in George Vernon's hand, and is almost

Edward Pierce carved the magnificent balustrade of the Great Staircase. The plasterwork ceiling was carried out by James Pettifer in 1675, and the oval painting by Laguerre was added in the 1690s to give the room a more fashionable Baroque character

Pierce's balustrade carving was based on engravings by his father, first published in 1640

certainly by him. On the other hand his account books record payments to a 'Mr. Whittricke, surveyor' of £100 in 1668 and a further £11 in 1671. He may have consulted William Fowler, a surveyor who worked for the family at that time. There is also the possibility that Vernon took advice on architectural matters from Sir William Wilson (1641–1710), the carver of the elaborate frontispieces at Sudbury in 1670. Wilson's designs for Four Oaks Hall, Sutton Coldfield, and for St Mary's church at Warwick, show something of the same curious mixture of Jacobean and classical ornament, as well as the same idiosyncratic window-frames.

Many of the ideas and details would have been derived from books and engravings – and indeed they have a strongly bookish look about them – but unfortunately there is no list of George Vernon's library, and so the sources are now extremely difficult to identify. He could have owned copies of Serlio and Palladio, both illustrated with woodcuts, but there were very few English prints available in 1660. It was not until 1674 that Robert Pricke produced his *Ornaments of Architecture* and *The Architect's Store-House,* which consisted largely of reworkings of engraved designs by such early seventeenth-century designers as Barbet and Francini. The rapid improvement in architectural and ornament design in England in George Vernon's time is directly related to a comparable improvement in the quality of architectural and ornament

illustration. And this is very apparent at Sudbury: there are obvious advances between the work of the early 1660s, of about 1670–2, and of about 1675–6. This is not just a matter of George Vernon's increasing knowledge and the greater skill of the men he employed later on, but it is also related to the availability of more sophisticated engraved sources of inspiration.

His own development is surely the explanation for why the upper parts of the exterior are more advanced in style than the lower. The actual shell took about five years to build and he may have modified the design after visits to London in the late 1660s. Indeed even the hipped roof may represent a change of mind. This is suggested by a comparison with Marchington Hall, a much smaller but more or less contemporary house a couple of miles across the valley: there, ridge roofs and gables appear over an otherwise typical Charles II façade. Perhaps George Vernon's first idea for Sudbury would have been a similar building with a gabled silhouette.

THE DECORATION OF THE HOUSE

If Ham House, near Richmond, is the most complete house of Charles II's reign as regards furniture and fabrics, Sudbury is now much the richest in terms of decoration. But it took a long time to complete, the finishing touches not being put to it until some twenty years after the roof was on. The most likely reasons for this were that George Vernon was building out of income and as the years passed, having learnt more, he became more exacting in his

The plasterwork ceiling in the Saloon was put up by the London craftsmen Bradbury and Pettifer in 1675

standards; also he may have lost the urge to carry on after the death of his first wife in 1675.

Whatever the reason for the slow pace, the decoration gives a gauge of the development of skill as well as style in the years after the Restoration. The men first employed were both more or less local. Samuel Mansfield, the plasterer who worked at Sudbury from 1672 to 1675, producing the rather stiff acanthus frieze in the Great Hall and on the ceiling of the Queen's Room, was a Derby man and as yet has not been found working anywhere else. Apart from his Sudbury work, he is remembered as the father of Isaac Mansfield, a leading *stuccadore* in the early eighteenth century, who was much used by James Gibbs. William Wilson, the carver responsible for the frontispieces on the two main fronts and for the alabaster chimneypiece and overmantel in the Queen's Room, was born in Leicester, and before he appears at Sudbury in 1676 is known to have worked at Lichfield Cathedral. Partly through his own skill and partly through the influence of his wife, a widow called Lady Pudsey, he was knighted in 1682 and went on to have a successful career as a carver and designer in the Midlands.

The mid-1670s were the main years of activity within the house after Wilson and Mansfield gave

way to London men: to Edward Pierce and Grinling Gibbons as carvers, and to Robert Bradbury and James Pettifer as plasterers.

Grinling Gibbons was paid £40 in 1678 to carve the swags of fish, game and fruit in the Drawing Room. He had been discovered by John Evelyn only seven years before and had yet to establish himself fully as the pre-eminent wood-carver of the era. Perhaps for that reason he was given nothing more to do at Sudbury. Edward Pierce, with whom Gibbons often worked, is a less famous, but equally interesting figure, for he combined carving with sculpting, contracting and designing. The son of a painter of the same name who worked at Wilton under Inigo Jones and John Webb, he is recorded as a mason at Horseheath Hall, near Cambridge, in 1665, and was closely involved with Christopher Wren's rebuilding of the City churches after the Great Fire in 1666. About the time he carved the luxuriant foliage for the balustrade of the Great Staircase and fitted out the Parlour (now the Saloon) at Sudbury, he was employed in the Chapel at Emmanuel College, Cambridge, by Archbishop Sancroft, and it was through the influence of the latter that he designed the Bishop's Palace at Lichfield in 1686. He also carved the staircase formerly at Wolseley Hall, Staffordshire. When Vernon's first wife died in 1675, he turned to Pierce to carve her monument in the church.

Less is known of Bradbury and Pettifer, the plasterers, and their reputation rests on their work at Sudbury, principally on the magnificent ceiling of the Long Gallery. James Pettifer is recorded as being employed at St Bride's, Fleet Street, and St James's, Piccadilly, and died in London in 1689.

In 1676 Vernon married Dorothy Shirley, the daughter of the staunch Royalist Sir Robert Shirley, who had built the church at Staunton Harold in Leicestershire during the Commonwealth, 'when all thinges sacred were throughout ye nation either demolisht or profaned'. Three years later, when the interior of Sudbury must have been nearing completion, he set out with her for London to buy new furnishings for the house. But their shopping expedition was overtaken by tragedy in March 1680, when Dorothy died in childbirth. George Vernon stayed in London to attend Parliament and, despite this second bereavement, continued to buy for Sudbury: paintings, tables, chairs and a chest-of-drawers, and an organ, communion table and altarpiece for the chapel.

Vernon went on tinkering with Sudbury into his old age. In the early 1690s he took on another London carver called Thomas Young, who later worked at Chatsworth. It is presumed that he carved the Parlour door at the foot of the Great Stairs. The arrival of the French decorative painter Louis Laguerre in 1691 also suggests a Chatsworth connection, which is not unlikely in view of the invitation to George Vernon to spend Christmas at Hardwick in 1680. Laguerre worked at Chatsworth from 1689 to 1694, and his ceiling paintings for the Saloon and Grand Staircase at Sudbury, for which he was paid between 1691 and 1694, appear as an attempt to bring up to date decoration that George Vernon may have felt was dropping out of fashion. The success of Laguerre and his Italian predecessor Antonio Verrio destroyed the trade of the Caroline plasterers in the end, but at Sudbury George Vernon tried to make his Caroline ceilings appear Baroque without removing them.

(Right) George, 1st Lord Vernon (1709–80) in hussar uniform; by Enoch Seeman, 1740 (no. 22; Saloon)

THE EIGHTEENTH CENTURY

George Vernon's new home was meant to become the proud seat of a dynasty, but although he produced fifteen children, the line almost ended with his death in 1702, as only one son survived him. Henry Vernon was not born until 1686, when his father had already buried two wives and was in his fifties. Henry's mother, Catherine Vernon, who was almost 30 years younger than his father, was the daughter of a rich London merchant and distant kinsman, and the sister-in-law of John Aislabie, who was to create the famous landscape garden at Studley Royal in Yorkshire. Henry Vernon followed the family tradition of marrying well. His first wife, Anne Pigot, was heiress not only to her father's property in Shropshire, but also to the valuable estates of her uncle, Peter Venables, at Kinder-

ton in Cheshire. For this reason, Henry and Anne's son, another George, changed his surname to Venables-Vernon on inheriting the Kinderton estates in 1715. Three years later he succeeded to Sudbury itself, where he was to reign for the next 62 years.

George Venables-Vernon believed that his ancient lineage, grand house, sizeable estates, and loyalty to the Crown during the Jacobite rebellion of 1745, entitled him to a peerage. In 1760 he badgered the Duke of Newcastle shamelessly for preferment: 'Pardon my saying that I think I have been of service, and may be of greater, as my interest in Derbyshire, Staffordshire, Cheshire, and Sussex are not inconsiderable, and his Majesty's

favour will strengthen them.' He was finally created the 1st Baron Vernon of Kinderton in 1762, thanks probably to lobbying by his brother-in-law, Lord Harcourt, who had been George III's governor when he was a child.

The house that Lord Vernon had inherited was old-fashioned even when new, and had 'some capital inconveniences from the largeness of the old-fashioned windows'. A bizarre, undated scheme to classicise Sudbury was produced, but nothing came of this, and the old mullioned windows were retained. However, he did decide to take down the wooden balustrade around the central platform of the roof and reduce the number of dormer windows, which were always weak points in such

George, 2nd Lord Vernon (1735–1813); by Thomas Gainsborough (Southampton City Art Gallery)

Georgiana Fauquier (1748–1823), who married the 2nd Lord Vernon in 1786; by John Hoppner (no. 30; Drawing Room)

Sudbury in the mid-eighteenth century, after the original roof balustrade had been removed (no. 36; Stone Passage)

roofs. (A similar process took place in the 1770s at another Restoration house, Belton in Lincolnshire.) The effect can be seen in an anonymous mid-eighteenth-century painting of Sudbury, illustrated above.

Lord Vernon, or his father, devoted more effort to improving the setting of the house. They swept away the formal approach on the north side and the garden on the south side that is shown in Griffier's painting and instead had great lawns running down to the new lake. On the north side an avenue was planted to frame the house, and across the road a large deer-park was laid out. The main feature of this was a huge Gothick deercote, in which deer could be penned, and which still stands about half a mile to the north of the house. It is said to have been built in 1723 and was certainly in existence by 1751.

A picture in the house (illustrated on p. 31) shows that it originally consisted of four corner towers capped by cupolas. Only traces of the plaster that once covered the red-brick walls now survive, and probably much of it had gone by the time the 'gate-house' was inserted, perhaps in the early nineteenth century.

Through his first wife, George, 2nd Lord Vernon, who succeeded his father in 1780, inherited substantial property in South Wales, including a country house at Briton Ferry in Glamorgan. His second wife, Georgiana Fauquier, was a formidable woman, who was painted in a full-length portrait by John Hoppner (now in the Drawing Room) and noticed by Horace Walpole in 1780:

> ... How I delight to see her
> Throw her broad black exterminating eye,
> And crush some new gilt courtier's loyal lie.

Vernon himself was known as the 'Hunting Lord' and was fond of exercising his hounds on the lawn between the house and the lake. Appropriately, when he was painted by Gainsborough in 1767, it was as a country gentleman with one of his dogs affectionately leaping up to greet him (the portrait was sold in 1919 and is now in the Southampton Art Gallery). He seems not to have sat to the best local artist of the time, Joseph Wright of Derby, who did, however, paint his musically minded agent, Stephen Jones, in 1785. As both Vernon's sons died in infancy, the family jewels and silver and Vernon House in London passed to his only daughter, Georgiana, who had married the 3rd Lord Suffield. Sudbury and the Vernon title went to his half-brother, Henry.

As his father's fourth son by his third wife, Henry, 3rd Lord Vernon can hardly have expected to inherit the estate in 1813, at the age of 66. To celebrate his good fortune, he had himself painted full-length in his peer's robes by the greatest portraitist of the age, Thomas Lawrence (the port-

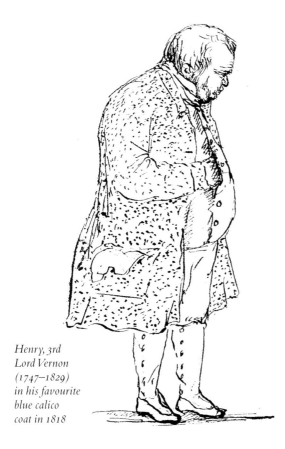

Henry, 3rd Lord Vernon (1747–1829) in his favourite blue calico coat in 1818

rait is now in the Great Hall). His youngest brother, Edward, began a distinguished clerical career as rector of Sudbury. He rose to become Archbishop of York, contributing substantial sums to the restoration of York Minster after the disastrous fires of 1829 and 1841. He also delivered the sermon at the Coronation of George IV in 1820, sternly warning that dissolute monarch against the 'contagion of vice'.

REVIVAL AND RETRENCHMENT

There has always been a certain naval tradition in the Vernon family. A distant cousin, Admiral Edward Vernon, had been an important advocate of reform in the early eighteenth-century navy; his nickname 'Old Grog' was applied to the sailors' favourite drink. George, 4th Lord Vernon married Frances Borlase Warren, the daughter of an admiral, and took a keen interest in naval affairs. He offered the Admiralty £50,000 to build a new type of 50-gun frigate, the sum to be forfeited if the vessel, christened HMS *Vernon*, was a failure. The ship, however, proved to be both fast and effective, and the money was returned. In 1826 he inherited, through his wife, the lucrative coalfields and cotton mills at Poynton in Cheshire. This seems to have encouraged him to embellish the garden at Sudbury, when he inherited the estate three years later, but work was interrupted by his death in 1835 (see p. 32). The 4th Baron died, fittingly, at sea, aboard his yacht *Harlequin* at Gibraltar. The body was brought back to Sudbury on her, and buried in the churchyard, with eight of his sailors acting as pall-bearers.

George, 5th Lord Vernon carried through a modest version of his father's plan for the garden. His son William, then aged four, remembered looking out of the Saloon window during the winter of 1837–8 as the new parterres were marked out with pegs and lengths of twine on the south lawn. Lord Vernon had more ambitious plans for the house. It was probably through Gilpin that he was introduced to the architect Anthony Salvin, who was collaborating at that time with Gilpin on a new house and garden at Scotney Castle in Kent. Salvin devised an extraordinary scheme to remodel

George, 5th Lord Vernon (1803–66) was a Dante scholar and crack shot: here he is shown competing in Basle in 1844

the exterior in a florid Jacobean style with Dutch gables, pinnacles and strapwork balustrades. Fortunately, Lord Vernon got cold feet, and restricted Salvin to building a new service wing to the east of the house and making internal changes, notably to the Great Hall, Library and Drawing Room. Lord Vernon also installed a rifle range at Sudbury, where he could practise his marksmanship: he was a crack shot and the winner of numerous competitions.

Because Lord Vernon was spending so much time in Italy, in the autumn of 1839 he decided to let Sudbury. For the next three years the house was rented out to William IV's widow, Queen Adelaide, in whose honour the Great Chamber of the Restoration house was renamed the Queen's Room, while Lord Vernon travelled on the Continent. For him this was no exile, as he had developed a love of

Italy in his youth, and was to spend most of his remaining years in Florence. He excavated Etruscan tombs near Cumae, and brought home a beautiful Etruscan necklace and numerous vases (some of the latter are now shown in the Library). He also became one of the leading Dante scholars of his generation. His finest achievement was what is known as the 'Vernon Dante'. These three sumptuous folio volumes contained his Italian prose version of the *Inferno*, an encyclopedia of Dantiana, and an album of related illustrations. According to a contemporary critic, 'for utility of purpose, comprehensiveness of design and costly execution, [it] has never been equalled in any country'. During his researches he created a superb collection of early Italian and French books, for which Salvin conceived a large new library adjoining the west front in 1857. Lord Vernon decided, however, on the cheaper option of new polished pine bookcases, which were installed all round the Long Gallery, with his Etruscan vases displayed on top.

The cotton shortages caused by the American Civil War of the 1860s devastated the Lancashire cotton industry, and also Lord Vernon's Poynton mills and collieries. Lord Vernon found himself losing £12,000 a year, and with 1,000 starving Cheshire employees and their families to support, which he did out of his own pocket. He was forced to economise, closing up the house again, and moving into 'the Cottage' in the village, the old home of his second wife, Fanny Boothby. He was too ill to participate in the celebrations for the 600th anniversary of Dante's birth in 1865, and died the following year. According to his son William, he was 'always a polished gentleman, and his natural kindness of heart made him beloved by all who really knew him. It was no effort to him to be courteous to *every*one'.

In the mid-1850s, while the 5th Lord Vernon was away in Italy, his son Augustus had moved into the house with his wife, Lady Harriet Anson, the daughter of the 1st Earl of Lichfield from Shugborough, across the border in Staffordshire. Of their ten children two died young in 1862 and are commemorated by a touching monument in the church. He redecorated the Long Gallery in 1864, and shortly after he succeeded as the 6th Lord

Vernon in 1866 he called in Salvin once more, who came up with an even more bizarre scheme to reconstruct the house in a Second Empire style. Fortunately, this was again rejected. In 1869 he turned to the son of the builder of the Houses of Parliament, E. M. Barry, who proposed erecting a massive tower with a tall mansard roof at the east end of the house. Barry also produced designs for a new stable block and for new servants' quarters in a neo-Jacobean style between the house and the stables. But Lord Vernon was happy with none of these proposals and dismissed Barry, probably in 1872. Despite all these setbacks, he looked around for another architect.

He may have been introduced to George Devey through Walter James of Betteshanger in Kent, who was one of this architect's most generous patrons and also Vernon's uncle by marriage. Devey rebuilt the roof, returned the dormer windows to their original appearance, and added a new stone balustrade at parapet level. On a photograph of the house taken in February 1873 while this work was underway, someone marked George Vernon's old balustrade in pencil, but Lord Vernon appears to have decided against reinstating it. Devey had a particular talent for creating new buildings in sen-

sitive old settings. He replanned Salvin's servants' quarters with two two-storey bays on the south side (the end bay was added in 1892), and recased them in red brick laid in diaper pattern to echo the Vernon fret pattern of the Restoration brickwork. Inside, Devey produced designs for the Oak Parlour, a new billiard-room, secondary stairs and hydraulic service lift, and created a new wing, which was not completed until after Lord Vernon's death.

Devey was also kept busy with a steady stream of work on the estate. He radically restored the church, adding new pinnacles (which were first mocked up in timber to show the effect). In Sudbury village he built new cottages, shops and a gasworks, which served the house, village, school and church – all in attractive neo-Jacobean brick. He also designed the Boar's Head pub at Sudbury station, and worked on Vernon's London house, 34 Grosvenor Street, and his Poynton colliery.

Lord Vernon struggled to maintain the estate in a grim period for agriculture. He was a conscientious contributor to the Royal Commission on Agriculture, and died shortly before he was due to give a major speech on the subject to the House of Lords in 1883. Although his son, George, 7th Lord Vernon, inherited almost £25,000 a year, he was soon in

The Long Gallery in 1904, when it still contained the 5th Baron's famous library and collection of Greek and Etruscan vases. The set of dining-chairs has recently returned to Sudbury, and is now on show in the Saloon

(Left) Sudbury in February 1873, while Devey's new parapet balustrade was being put up and the roof rebuilt. Someone has pencilled on to the photograph the original balustrade, but this was not put back

financial difficulties. He tried to bolster the estate in the familiar way by marrying an heiress, in his case an American, Frances Lawrance. With her money he was able to put in hand repairs to the old stables, complete Devey's wing and build a new stable block and coach-house. The work was carried out by the Sudbury clerk of works Theodosius Coxon in 1892–4. But Lord Vernon became very ill and was forced to let the house to the Gretton brewing family during the last years of the century. When he died in 1898 at 44, he was living in a villa in Bournemouth.

His elder son and heir, another George, belonged to that doomed generation whose youth coincided with the First World War. In 1916, aged only 28, he died of dysentery contracted while on active service in Gallipoli. His younger brother, who served in the Royal Navy, survived the war. After a period of retrenchment and absence, in 1922 the 9th Lord Vernon returned to live at Sudbury, which was to be his home for the next 41 years. He and his wife Violet commissioned the fashionable London firm of Lenygon & Morant to carry out a programme of redecoration and reorganisation of the contents, which had been necessitated partly by the sales of books, pictures and furniture in 1918 and 1919. So, for instance, the Drawing Room was redecorated in 'a pleasant May blue Hampton Court paper'. *Country Life* illustrated the results of their efforts in a series of articles written in 1935 by Christopher Hussey, who drew new attention to the importance of the house and its largely untouched Restoration plasterwork and carving.

THE NATIONAL TRUST

After the 9th Lord Vernon's death in 1963, the house and its principal contents were offered by his son to the Treasury in payment of death-duties and transferred to the National Trust in 1967 through the National Land Fund. The 10th Lord Vernon built himself a new house on the estate, which was designed by Sir Martyn Beckett in 1965 and which remains the home of his daughter and her family. Without a capital endowment (apart from a sum generously given by Lord Vernon), the cost of restoring and redecorating Sudbury Hall had to

be met by the Historic Buildings Council and Derbyshire County Council, which created the Museum of Childhood in the Devey wing in 1974.

The task of redecorating the house fell to a small group consisting of the Duchess of Devonshire, James Lees-Milne, Christopher Wall and John Fowler. They had two main aims: to make the most of the original carving and plasterwork which are the glory of Sudbury; and to use colour to compensate for the relative lack of furniture. There was no question of showing the house as furnished in the seventeenth century by George Vernon, and they were in any case anxious to retain the mellow, probably nineteenth-century, paint on the walls of the Saloon and the Long Gallery. Different tones of white were used to pick out the plasterwork, with greater contrasts reserved for the richer ceilings. The most dramatic change was on the Staircase, where the balustrade, previously painted chocolate brown, was stripped and painted white, with the walls a vivid yellow. The dark polish was also taken off the floorboards in the principal rooms.

The new scheme provoked considerable controversy at the time, and still has its critics among those who remember the house as it used to be. So it is perhaps worth quoting John Fowler's rationale for his approach:

Of course all attempt to play up the character of the decoration could have been resisted, and the whole place could have been frozen, but particularly in a sparsely furnished house like Sudbury, whose sole use is to be shown to visitors, the impact on those visitors must be considered and they must be given an experience that is as rich and enjoyable as possible. It is a matter of degree how far one goes in this, but there must be some compensation for the loss of contents over the years and that living feeling that inevitably goes when the family moves out. However, at the same time whatever is done must not lose touch with either reality or credibility. There can be no absolute and timeless answer to such problems, and each generation will restore country houses in different ways just as they will redecorate them in different ways. Indeed it is to be hoped that the element of decoration will continue to influence approaches to restoration. Then at least there will be striving after a sense of life and not just slavish renewal of the misguided taste of the day before yesterday.